BALLOON
POP
OUTLAW
BLACK

PATRICIA
LOCKWOOD

BALL

PO

OUT

BLA

OCTOPUS
BOOKS

OON

OP

AW

CK

PORTLAND   DENVER   OMAHA

BALLOON POP OUTLAW BLACK

PUBLISHED BY OCTOPUS BOOKS
WWW.OCTOPUSBOOKS.NET

COPYRIGHT © 2012 PATRICIA LOCKWOOD
ALL RIGHTS RESERVED

ISBN 978-0-9851182-2-8
FIRST EDITION

OCTOPUS BOOKS IS DISTRIBUTED BY SMALL PRESS DISTRIBUTION
WWW.SPDBOOKS.ORG

PRINTED BY THOMSON-SHORE, INC. IN THE UNITED STATES

COVER ART BY LISA HANAWALT
WWW.LISAHANAWALT.COM

DESIGNED & SET BY DREW SCOTT SWENHAUGEN
TITLE FONT SET IN CHAMPAGNE & LIMOUSINES
BODY FONT SET IN A VERSION OF CASLON

WHEN WE MOVE AWAY FROM HERE, YOU'LL SEE A CLEAN SQUARE OF PAPER WHERE HIS PICTURE HUNG

THE CARTOON'S MOTHER BUILDS A HOUSE IN HAMMERSPACE

THE QUICKENING

ACKNOWLEDGMENTS

For Jason, without whom this entire book
would have been written in a trashcan

WHEN WE MO

HERE, YOU'LL

SQUARE OF P

PICTUR

E AWAY FROM

SEE A CLEAN

PER WHERE HIS

HUNG

WHEN WE MOVE AWAY FROM HERE, YOU'LL SEE A CLEAN SQUARE OF PAPER WHERE HIS PICTURE HUNG

The oldest living cartoon character is the word "popeye." A cartoon character works this way: it is written so many times, with minor variations, that it appears to walk, to cast a shadow, to eat green leaves. Here are the known facts:

His pants are not white, they are empty. His face is not white, it is empty. His arms are not white, they are empty. When we say "pants, face, arms" what we mean is "where the ink ends and the rest of him begins," or, "the him that the ink contains."

His parts are letters. Letters make up his mind, and also emerge from it. And the point where a needle touches his thought bubble to burst it is a letter also.

When he fights his number-one enemy, he undergoes a transformation: he smiles hugely, his teeth turn to rows of movable type, and then rearrange themselves to form an ultimate insult. The enemy then begins to cry, and "popeye" is the winner.

He does not eat, exactly, but the existence of bite-marks in pen-and-ink apples is enough to keep him from going hungry. "Grainy," he often complains.

When he develops goosebumps, when he forms a knot on the head, when his legs fly apart and form a fast-moving cloud, his line suffers. When his line suffers, it is said that he is "in pain." Whenever he is "in pain," a doctor appears and injects him with a straight line, and he sighs with relief.

Much as gold injections are used to treat lions with arthritis.

He has never worn a mustache, because he is not capable of growing a mustache. This is because he lacks both the letters M and W.

What does "popeye" mean? The doctor swabs the inside of his cheek and smears it on a slide, and looks and looks and looks.

He wakes one morning with amnesia, and when one doctor asks his name, and another doctor asks if he knows where he is, he will only say slowly, "My name is 'popeye,' I have no other English."

"POPEYE": AN OUTLINE

1. Opening: First draw him a mouth, to ask "who, what, when, where, why, and how?" Then fill the mouth with ink.

2. The Body: Think of your paper as a pan of milk. A pan of milk will form a skin.

3. Closing: There is a small gap between where the arm of "popeye" ends and the fist of him begins. Please join them with your pen.

Eyebrows are his most expressive feature. He himself, straightened, is someone's eyebrow.

In moments of grave danger, his bicep turns transparent, and reveals a sizable ink-clot, with small rivers of ink streaming away from it to form his outline, day after day, year after year. This is to reassure his viewers, who continually fear his death.

"Popeye," in his adolescence, goes through a period of floating off the page. His father sits him down and recommends an anchor tattoo.

Although he is "drawn," and although he is "a place," he is not a map. If anything, he is a "cartouche": the area of a map that encloses information about the map itself.

He is often captured and sentenced to slave labor, always the same: to row oars in other moving words, and be whipped within an inch by ascenders and descenders.

Watching him works this way: he walks the length of your vision until he reaches the end. You gulp like a gangplank and he falls into the Drink.

Or: He disappears into the sunset, riding a little
killie over and under the waves.

Or: His enormous boyfriend is named Perspective;
he ties him to train tracks again and again.

Any piece of paper on which "popeye" is printed counts as a Will, as it contains his signature, his witness, proof of his death, a list of all the property he owns, and the name of his inheritor.

Occasionally a schoolgirl will write "popeye" over and over with a pink pen, and it is then that he wears a dress and pretends to be a lady.

Depending on the decade, draws seams up the backs of his legs.

Parts of his body exist only when he is looking at them. He uses his shoeshine to stare up his own skirt.

At the school dance, "popeye" feels a pang in his belly and an urge to push. "Why me?" he wonders. "Why now?" Alone, he disappears through the door marked & and does what he must do.

When he is angry, a frizz of black ink appears above his head. No, forgive me. That is not ink at all. That is the least favorite hair of the typesetter, the one that emerges from the thought of his mother.

THE ONGOING CRIMES OF HIS MOTHER AND FATHER

His mother reaches out, hatches ink under him,
and commands him to stand and walk.

His father bursts into the room, screaming,
"What is the meaning? What is the meaning
of this?"

His mother rushes to explain, and feels
the pain of a strikethrough fly through her.

"Popeye" famously wets himself—the worst
mistake a young image can make.

His father lifts a ruler, brings it down hard
on his "boy," lifts a paint-stirrer up again.

"Popeye" is an extension of the human arm. When driving horses, lift and crack him until your horses break into a black streak. Then set him upright in the whip socket again.

He is famous for being always on time; he arrives at his destination in one second flat.* In one minute flat. In one hour flat.**

     *How? We suspect that he lives in an atlas, where all distances are collapsible.

          **"Flat" is not the word. Say instead, there is a limited amount of him, like water, and it seeks its level.

Is he "made of paper"? No, he is papered like a hallway. Is he "made of ink"? No, he is a ghost who had ink thrown on him during a fight, and as a consequence is now visible.

Regarding ink, why black? Black because something was extinguished there?

When rain falls on him, it falls in interruptions, incompletes, broken-offs and bitten-backs—it is true to its typographical nature and never touches the ground.

Every second Sunday, his mother combs kerosene through his hair. The lice that live on books are not the same as the lice that live on scalps, and "popeye" has them both.

Occasionally he is left unfinished—that is, winter comes and snows in the page while his mother still has three fingers left to knit.

A poster called "Phases of the Moon" is tacked on the schoolroom wall. It shows his face in shadow, half in shadow; in light, half in light.

Page by page the "popeye" calendar is torn away. Page by page he is sent through the shredder, and finds himself in long days like the year.

"Popeye" goes hunting and brings down a 12-pointer. He drags the body to a clearing. "Thought bubble, thought bubble," he says meditatively, and eats the lungs.

Were you a carnivore before you saw him? You are a carnivore now. He is served in slices. He is served bone-in and skin-on.

While he sleeps, "popeye" dreams of being eaten by the lion, the tiger, the leopard, the jaguar. All the roaring cats appear to him, and he dreams of being spoken backward through their strong black lips.

And being reborn on their backs as: a pattern on a solid-color coat.

And being shot, skinned, and laid out on a library floor. And his mouth forced open to seem always to be speaking.

"Popeye" stars in a revival of *A Sensation Novel*. He stands on a bare stage and delivers everyone's lines. Between acts, all-in-black move back and forth and break down the scenery behind him.

The purpose of a shadow is: to put "popeye" where he is not. Shadowed he stands, like a stencil letter, always next to himself.

His protruding "pop-eye" is a world-ending button. When its dark outline disappears, you will know that the button is being pressed.

His other eye a crow walked closed.

"Popeye" loves all literature; he keeps hens for their scratchings and chickens for their prints.

One flipbook depicts him walking out to his garden and watering his own buried body until a white cabbage grows from him and prettily presents its outer leaves. This book is perpetual, and flips back and forth continually.

This flipbook is so thick that even the strongman cannot tear it. Instead, he tears a phonebook filled only with the names of "popeye" and his descendants, and the page numbers that are their addresses.

> (Of sick numbers, it is said, "Number one is: number one on the list for a transplant; number two is: number two on the list." The first and oldest "popeye" waits for his living donor to appear, and takes comfort in the knowledge that there is no death in his phonebook, and there are no unlistings.
>
> Picture his impossible funeral: hundreds of him, laid out in the little coffins of the prepositions: under under, over over. In in.)

So many mouths to feed! In a permanent kitchen, in a permanent corner, he stretches a single meal as far as it will go. Slices and slices a transparent pie.

After supper, he sits on the porch with a long black shotgun and waits for a buffalo to wander into view. He uses every part of the buffalo—he uses them down to their eyewhites, he uses the very lines that make them up.

He walks to the city to be counted in the census. A wind gets itself up and ruffles him relentlessly, but miniature monuments hold him down.

His paper is usually neatly stacked, especially when still in original trees.

Lives where? In voices: hills and valleys. Lives all in the alphabet as if it were a rowhouse. Lives at the peak of the tallest chalk hill.

> Or lives: nowhere at all. He wanders the desert, written on old skins, moaning, "Where is home, where is home?" And waits for a tent peg to be driven through his skull.

He walks to the edge of his very country, he walks forward till he fills his profile completely, he walks into the water of Marblehead.

"Popeye" sits on the riverbank and sends himself sailing into the water: he is a good graphite rod with a strong fly line; he sings away from his reel.

His occasional girlfriend, doodled in the margins, cannot have intercourse with him; she suffers badly from vestibulitis.

A disorder of her entrance.

She faints every time he tries. "Popeye" reads the dictionary out loud to revive her. He reads, "Syncope is: a blackout, a loss of consciousness. Syncope is: the loss of one or more sounds from the interior of a word."

While her eyes are closed, he must suppress the temptation to spread her out and pin her like a map through a single place. For her skirt is cut to here, her blouse is cut to there!

NOTES ON HIS MOVEMENT

He is photographed in the still old style, wearing
a shirt patterned with white cartwheels.

His pants patterned with instructions for a two-step.

The old music players have a strong solid base like the base of a statue, and a flowering-
out above. A statue of "popeye" rises in the center of the song that is playing:

Popeye the man is no longer standing!
Popeye the man has been killed in the stomach;
his French horn spills out and out!

"Popeye" drops from the sky. The townspeople gather to watch him fall and wait to see
his imprint in the pavement, but he reaches out at the last moment and grabs a branch—
of what?—of the clock tower. He is suspended there still, hanging off the hour hand.

Or:

In a town with no clock tower, "popeye" falls from a great height and his thigh-bones are driven up into his body, click, like the first length of lead in a mechanical pencil.

Or:

Past, present, and future: "popeye" falls in a painting. In the foreground, a farmer pays no attention, and binds bales of newspapers in a field. "Popeye" will limp to him later, and ask to be splinted with rolled-up dailies.

> (A broken leg is often fatal for a "popeye;"
> one blank to the temple will take him out.)

If the dailies succeed in prolonging him, he will heal into a new configuration: his body will bend and twist and seize; he will become a living monk's cramp.

"Popeye" is the priest, and you must confess to him. There is a black grate where his face should be.

What does he worship—the Cross or the Clean Line? The churches here have lines for the pews to sit in, and the Bible here is Dürer's hare.

And who is his higher power? From time to time, he feels the glass hover above him, feels magnified, feels "read," and feels it move away.

Believes he walks on a beach, but above him, a lens is ground and ground.

And what was broken open to reveal him? In his world, all visible things stand up on the half-shell.

> Correction: "I do not live in a world at all," "popeye" says indignantly, and tightens the equator around his waist.

And does he fear death? He dreams he is a brand that sits in the fire forever.

It is impossible to know when he was born. A fragment dating from 500 BC refers to him; the title is translated as "Popeye Wavers a Little in the Heat," or alternately, "Popeye Lives in a Hell of Line Boil." Many have attempted to translate:

> A pencil ship is difficult to wreck, but "popeye"
> manages every time. The sun shines directly
> above him, he floats on a raft of reflection
> all the way to shore. He is caught. Cannibals
> carry him home on a pole, and cannibals
> cook him alive in worst-hot sketch-water.
> > He lives in every mouth now,
> > he cannot call himself his own!

Or:

A ship drawn only with parallel lines will never
reach its destination, and will sink if it sinks
only straight down. "Popeye" sails for the horizon
because it is all he can see: he lacks the vertical
stroke I. He sails and he sails, tied to the mast,
> the ocean boiling over below him,
> feeling his own head turn to a ham,
> feeling slices turn over one by one.

A long book of him is called a "brick," and a long book of him is called a "doorstop."

When it came time to put these pages in order, I laid them all out on the floor, creating the appearance of a city of rooftops seen from above. And "popeye," who lived there, had climbed to each one.

And lay on his back reading "The Myth of the Bookcover."

And stood up like a writing tendon, and said, "Why did you leave the book open? Anyone could have walked in."

THE WEST READS HORIZONTAL TEXT

And reads it west to east. The west reads horizontal
text: the people in our long black lines lie down before
they lie down for good, they float on their backs and watch
       the weather, and the weather learns to read, so read:

A LIMP-COVER NOVEL:

"Two women are bathing in an elbow of the river;
then a thunderclap heard by no one comes; then it is raining
directly and always into the names Anna and Emma..."

OR A LEATHER HISTORY:

"Two men are bathing in a belly of the river;
then they are lit by lightning; then it is raining directly
and always into the names Cotton and Increase..."

The water washes them drop by drop. The water believes
we have, like sardines, a general not a specific body.
The water dries on legs and arms, and rises in the air,
and rides across itself to other countries. Now it rains
into the name of the taxonomist's little mother. It is filling
up her form. Her eyes roll so far north, she begins to see
       great white...whats? She will dry and return,
    she will bead on their backs. She drinks and thinks
        what she will call the first animal.

KILLED WITH AN APPLE CORER, SHE ASKS
WHAT DOES THAT MAKE ME

For all her life she did piece work
on the orange assembly line, she tied
awful flesh knots at the ends of oranges
to separate one from the next,

> (her father was the same, her father
> squinted at blueprints of bulls, and built
> them up room by room, and then sent
> them into the fields
> > to graze on pure
> > thousands instead of the grass,)

she lived in the squarest state, she was soft
as map creases are, her lover, one floor
above, worked to make things themselves:
steel driven home in steel and shoehorns
shoehorned in, he lost piece by piece
> his whole body that way;

> until she no longer wanted him
> and took a lover one floor below
who brought game after game to life—when she
told him, "The forest is as tall as a paper mill
tonight," he took her walking there, and they
envisioned each tree as a bundle of cues, or horse-
heads set on endless Ls, or a deep sleeve of letter tiles.
And when he was unlucky too, he climbed upstairs
and raised a right arm that suddenly seemed to be
missing,
> and cried, "Machine beats man," and finally
fell at her feet, his wounds pouring red rolls of the dice;

and then using her terrible skills, she tied him off from her,
and then went to the man who made things themselves
and lay down on his line, and he said her name
like industrial noise but finally it meant nothing,

and "What is happening?" she asked,
and he leaned down and told how the air
          drilled a hole in her to breathe,
and he leaned down and told how the red
             spiraled off in one neat piece,

THE MOUTH OF THE ANTHILL IS LEARNING TO WRITE

Loops of honey are laid out all over the face
of the earth; lines of ants find one and then
another, and travel over them solidly and
do not stop;
      everywhere forms fall jam-
side down and everywhere ants discover them
and outline them in black. A man lifts one
of three shells to find a seething ball of ants,
continually
            writing "pea, pea, pea;"

      they are everywhere in his landscape,
thirsty, their perfect displacements swim
through dark depictions of rivers, he walks
      home manned with a million of them
and they draw his footprints two by two;

and they march his line of vision, they march
a level view, they march his paper route
and they arc onto his lawn, they climb up
to his weathervane and eat NSWE. All
      their black belongs inside keyholes
      and all of a piece they open the door;

"Always on the dot," he says, and they eat four o'clock
      off the wall. They tell him time for tea, and stir
      themselves into his cup, they are particulate
within their word as sugar, they settle to the bottom
of the cup still thirsty
      and drink a design of two doves,
delicious—it tastes like blue water from bird tracks
they say. He stares and a plural endearment
rises in his mind, how he misses his long-gone
Sweetness, so granular within her single word,
      and all of a piece they become his pet, they lick,
      they eat a pencil lead out of the palm of his hand,

and write lines of us will outlast
you, when you no longer have any form
we will eat you off your own portrait
plate; when the earth no longer has surface
          we will eat it off willow-pattern,
and when that is finished, two by two,
                    we will eat Love Scene itself.

HISTORY OF THE HOUSE WHERE YOU WERE BORN

First it was the house where you were born—
born tragically, with an Appearance—and so
many people crowded to see that the house
mistook them for hungry, and you balanced
your reflection on the blade of a knife
and said, "I have slices to sell them,"
   and the house where you were born
     became a butcher-slash-
window store,
   where squares of glass were carved
one by one off the clear animal itself. Your father
the butcher took huge joy in riding out on the plains,
out into railroad country, ignoring all warm blood
in his path, and staring instead at sparse escaped
herds of black Observation Cars, who grazed on
what grass there was. He shot them and carried
them home on his shoulder, and you grew up loving
strong wild strips of them. Their numbers dwindled,
the survivors grew smaller, and he was forced to sell
their skins for spectacles instead. Then nothing was
left but the gold and black bones, and he hung them
and called it a frame store. You never saw clearly before,
surrounded by flashing glass, so lift your head and look
   around: your landscape is taken over by Frame Store,
    Frame Store as far as the eye can see.

The frames hang straight and still know nothing.
They believe they are still the body of their animal,
strung and stood up with wire, filled with fat
organs of baby looks. The walls of the frame store
are worse: they were given good coats of white;
they felt paint stroked on and knew what they were:
"I feel hundreds of buffalo nudes being driven off
a cliff," proclaims the whitest one. Another, even
whiter, feels paint that paint puts on: rouged cheeks
in a row, silver frost

on fruit, and rainbows on raw meat.
One feels, still on the palette, blood next to clear blue sky.

And all feel glass panes everywhere.
And you are the butcher now; you wipe
blood on your blue apron. Then the walls
that surround you know they are white,
            are sure they feel a picture
of the knife-sharpener finally going too far.

THE CARTOON

A HOUSE IN

MOTHER BUILDS

AMMERSPACE

THE CARTOON'S MOTHER BUILDS A HOUSE
IN HAMMERSPACE

The dimension is a coat; it is flowered on green ground. The cartoon wouldn't wear it if his mother didn't force him.

The coat has deep pockets, and the cartoon is compelled to reach into them—to a baby's thumb, everything looks like a mouth.

The cartoon reaches deep into a pocket, deep into a hole in the pocket, into "hammer-space," and retrieves a huge pair of scissors. His mother, who lives there, hands him what he needs. Touches the tips of his fingers.

> (She spends so much time alone, lifting a hammer and bringing it down, that she has come to think of *herself* as a house. This hand is the first door on her right, that hand is the first door on her left, and she passes objects through them.)

Meanwhile, the enemy's hair keeps growing out of nowhere, pulling itself further into existence minute by minute.

The cartoon cuts it as fast as it can grow, cuts it closer and closer to the head, then disappears under his enemy's scalp and snips the very idea of hair. Which will grow again.

When the cartoon wants a well-fitting suit of clothes, he lifts a square of cloth and forces himself through it, and emerges on the other side fully dressed.

SHE DIVES INTO A PUDDLE OF SILK ON THE STAGE

The mother, as naked as any woman and nakeder than some, tried the same trick and ended up here. She chose the wrong cloth, or what she chose was not cloth at all, or the cloth she chose did not like to be clothes.

Or was she so unseemly that he hid her away? Why not let me stay? she wonders. I wouldn't take much space. A ball and chain can learn to hide behind the barest line of leg.

When she arrived, she looked more put-together than usual. She was suddenly wearing a small blue hat on her head like a neat splash into water.

When the cartoon undresses at night, he walks back through the square of cloth, makes it whole again, and tucks himself in with it.

He sleeps with his top-hat on, since he so often dreams of his enemy. It is a dream he loves: the enemy rushes at him, and knocks the top-hat off his head, and punches the top-hat of his thinking through, and he wakes.

The circles of black cloth come flying into her sky and float there, trailing their long threads down. She moves among their shadows; she stares up at their undersides; the world is as lidded as a lily pond.

Sometimes he prefers not to touch her. Then she feels a tug like her "tooth" is tied to a string, and she follows the line of the string to the door, and watches as the door is yanked open, and the "tooth" that he needs goes flying toward him.

How can she always arrive at him? Her own mother confessed she was the mailman's.

SHE IS THE BLOND HANDLE OF AN AX*

She moves as smoothly as the moment of a mousetrap, and
when her cartoon needs a mousetrap she gives one to him.

Even the act of extending an arm toward him produces a trombone.

And as she watches herself extend an arm, a collapsible
spyglass leaps out of her eye.

When she tiptoes across the lawn, so does a small green rosebush.

When a wrecking ball swings out of nowhere, she is riding it;
she makes a round cutout in the enemy's house and then
rides the cutout home.

Imagine her body as a barrel of gunpowder, uncorked,
spilling black along the ground behind it.

When she spreads her arms and sinks down, she brings a
detonator into the world.

Her measurements are ideal: they are the combination to the family safe.

Is he even still her son? If a cartoon holding an ax has had his ax-handle replaced once and his ax-head replaced twice, is he still the same cartoon?

   *A handle consists of throat, belly and grip.

He is not ungrateful; he pulls coins from behind his ear to pay her. She takes them, still warm from her hand.

Sometimes an object is altered when it enters his world, becomes bigger or smaller, changes color or develops impossible angles. Some tools even grow an elbow to wield themselves with, as a ray of light grows an elbow when it enters water.*

   *As vision is given an elbow when it enters a periscope.**

Inseparable things are easily separated, she knows. The name of the tea at one end of the string, the tea itself at the other.

   **And out-of-frame elbows connect arms with arms.

Even here, she can feel when he winds up to throw a fastball. Inside her own arm feels the setting of a sleeve.

Allow me to sketch some background behind her—a person made of paper is only as fat as her file.

When he was young, she suffered an excess of connective tissue. Suffered from/with and and and.

The house where he grew up was full of the marks of her illness—connection was everywhere. She threw handfuls of three-hole-punches in the air on his birthday; she threw the whole year's worth.

Tossed balls of rubber bands to him. And in the hallway, drops of her blood on the floor like sealing wax.

In the garage, she asked her son for wrench after wrench, and one by one they materialized in her hand. She never looked away from her work, and after a long time came to believe that the endless stream of wrenches *was* her son, and she laid them out smallest to largest, and tucked a row of them in at night, and in the end loosened everything she owned with them.

When she first landed here, she wandered for a while, living out of her own two pockets, until one day she came upon a square of lawn the size of a handkerchief. Below, from another world, the idea of a house was forcing itself upward, trying to come out on the other side clothed.

A chandelier already hanging in the middle of the sky.

The flowers all in clear vases.

A slot in the air for mail. Even a peephole. And a crack through which someone was saying, Who is it, what do you want?

She sets a rectangular stone in the middle of the lawn. It must be a doorstep, because she finds a fawn there the very next morning. She carries him "inside," and feeds him with an eyedropper full of milk. He stays with her for a long while, and then one day he walks "outside" and begins paying his white spots one by one into a slot in the air, and disappears, and emerges in the other world as a fully grown deer.

(How is this possible? Flatness disappears into a gumball machine; roundness rolls out.)

She watches him go, and then falls asleep on the doorstep. She wakes hungry, because what did she eat for a year? She ate the milk that she dropped into the fawn.

A year has gone by without her noticing—time does not flow smoothly here, but grows in bunches like bananas. After a while, she stops looking at her wrist. She is alone, this is no island, and no day of the week will ever walk by.

Food is not the same here either. She reaches out and wrenches down a good year for apples, and eats it noisily, and meanwhile studies her surroundings.

Equal lengths of board grow out of the ground, shingle beaches stretch on and on, and yellowhammers live here.

The animals all live in hollow trees, or disappear down holes exactly the size of their bodies, or go for daily fittings in blue water.

Which came first? she wonders. As she begins to imagine the house, she feels whole rooms added on to herself, bays and gables, east and west windows, a crawlspace and a fireplace, a rolling ladder in a library. An attic forces its way up, a white stone walkway leads to her.

At night, she stares up at the place where her roof will be, where horizontal and vertical lay thatch above her.

She doesn't start building right away—she sleeps on the doorstep at night and runs wild during the day. With no one watching, she feels no need to be decent. Wears only enough of a skirt to clean her spectacles with.

Captures the cloth herself. In the other world, no one ever skins an animal for the parts that are actually useful, like for instance the backs of their eyelids.

From time to time she remembers the fawn, and tries to pay the brown coins on the back of her hands through the slot, but it will not take them.

She twists up her black and white hair. Her chignon seems almost to open a portal into the back of her head, right onto the idea of hair.

A pencil speared through it, to hold it in place.

As her idea of hair grows longer, she starts stacking it higher every day, first to make room for bird wings, then to make room for whole birds, then to make room for their cages.

And when the cages are large enough to live in, she begins to build.

She finds a place where the ground seems least solid, and begins to lay her floor. The floor moves with the ground under it—when she closes her eyes, she is stepping across a stream on the tiled backs of turtles.

The tape measure merges into her hand; inches leap out when she attempts to point a finger. Why couldn't this happen in the other world? she agonizes. This hand would be easier for him to hold.

She sets her hammer on the windowsill to cool, and the smell of it rises up and reaches out to him.

She wonders how big the rooms should be, and where exactly the walls should go. She walks over every inch of the floor, trying to feel when she is half-in and half-out.

She knows where the baseboards should be; the mouseholes are already in place.

In the nearby desert, there are round splashes of glass where meteorites struck the sand. She goes window-gathering there.

The ladders she leans against the half-finished house seem to become part of it. As soon as she leans one, it stays, until the look of the house is all ladders—light and dark wood, and gleaming metal, and plaid shadow. They reach into the ground and sprout new leaves above, rustling green and rattling tin.

Likewise, the paint cans that she leaves out on the lawn screw themselves down into the grass, and allow hummingbirds to dive into them, and arrest themselves in the act of splashing up.

It's hard to tell where the house ends and outside begins—the surroundings of the house almost seem to hold it up. And it's hard to tell where the house ends and her insides begin, there is so much inside around her. As if a house could be eaten, as if a house could eat her.

It is the house of your childhood: rooms hide, merge, relocate, paint themselves during the night. The same route never works twice—you are the force that sends a live hallway shooting out of another hallway. There is a never-ending bowl of oranges in the kitchen, always the same oranges and never the same oranges; the oranges section and eat the weeks. The dog's markings—black on white ground—change whenever we want them to. Some seasons the lawn disappears out from under you like a tablecloth, and you're replaced so fast you hardly feel it. And it is the house of your childhood because she lives here.

In the kitchen, one cupboard refuses to open. It thinks it is another place, it thinks it is the land of spices.

A house in Kansas is made of Kansas. A house in the jungle is made of the jungle. The house here is made of there, is made of the air that a house displaces.

Her garden flourishes: a row of little signs that say pumpkin, a row of little signs that say lettuce, a row of little signs that say radish.

When she wants to pick one, she gets down on her knees and grasps the name with both hands, and tugs, and it will not come, and tugs, and it will not come, and in the other world her son cries "Carrot!" and she feels the taproot go tense and then snap.

It is a good place to grow things; the thermometer on the front porch registers always a human temperature.

Last thing she knew he lived in the west. When his name appears in her mind, it is written in lasso.

He always liked a good lie about storms, so here, when it thunders, a stampede of horses is flattening her son.

And in the morning her trails are washed away. The ground here is a dapple animal, it won't stand still long enough to let her pull a bridle path over its head.

And where is the west now? She tugs down the map to look and it flies up again like a windowshade.

At the edge of the desert, she discovers a rich vein of Detroitite—a "stone" made of the layered paint that streams away from car factories. She takes a pickaxe and a shovel and begins to dig. She dynamites the color deeper and deeper. She lives away from home, she rides a gray donkey down, she eats sandwiches in the mine at night. It is her Grand Canyon, and she sleeps in a long silver river at the bottom. Above her, new layers keep arriving; they will run here from the other world as long as there is somewhere to go.

Then the vein is inside out, and she wakes up one morning in her own bed again. The house is suddenly one floor deeper, she feels a room of basement rocks below her.

One shop appears when she needs it: a model train store. It sells everything a town needs, from portable tunnels to instant road, but she lingers most over the miniature "You Are Now Entering _____ " signs. They have one for every city you can think of, piled together in a clear glass jar. She slips one in her pocket and lets it burn a hole there.

When she wants to travel, she sits on a bench in the middle of nowhere. The scenery train pulls out. The scenery train pulls in. When her ticket is right, she will leave on it, and ride to the end of the line.

She is always on the lookout for lines here; the line is her only natural predator. If she let it, a line would swallow her whole and then lick the corner of her lip, and lay in a black earthquake on her floor, and draw itself in black boxes all over her calendar. It would ride out to her yard and draw tree full of grasshoppers until there was not a leaf left, and still not be full. The line says, "When I draw a stomach around all of it, then I will have eaten."

Her son keeps a line, she remembers, and feeds it a mouse once a month. As soon as the mouse is fully digested, it appears here in her house, a long tail snaking behind it.

Sometimes a line disguises himself, and goes house to house with a paper and pen asking for signatures. She refuses to answer. He raps, then knocks, then threatens to put a shoulder through her door.

She sends her son a book, with her pop-up house between the pages. He sets it aside and lets it gather dust. She raps, then knocks, then threatens to put her shoulder through the door, but still he does not open it.

She brought all her books with her, too many books. She makes bookends to hold rows of them together: geodes the size of her head, sawed exactly in half, all gray crystals on display.

> The line would like to cut her up and hang her from the ceiling. If he did, you would see a clean white portal in each piece, like a hambone. She is tempted to let him do this—like all good cartoons, she believes in an Afterimage, where her colors will become their cool opposites. Where her hell-colored ham will become the blue sky.

She keeps a Bible by her bedside, called *Parallel Worlds for Children!* It begins, "Imagine a stair tree, nearly as wide as it is tall, with ripe clear chandeliers hanging among the leaves. Imagine that the tree is hollow, and imagine that a bolt of lightning strikes permanently down the middle, in steps, and it does not hurt you to climb them. This is your house; you live here. When you want to go down the roots descend in steps, and when you want to go out the branches are banisters, and when you want to go in, there's a knothole halfway up the tree that is a tight coil of stairs. (Take a candle, and cast smaller and smaller selves on the wall as you go, and finally turn inside out, and let your father and mother turn their pockets inside out to bury you.) And when you want to go up, let the rooms grow smaller as you climb, and let yourself grow smaller as you climb, until finally the A of your pointed head approaches the A of the pointed roof, and fits there for a moment, and the roof raises off. And it feels like nothing else. Like arriving at the tip of a perfectly sharpened pencil."

She imagines herself arriving at the tip of a perfectly sharpened pencil, and then imagines the pencil sketching out a safe, a mousetrap, a hundred-pound weight.

She imagines it drawing a pair of huge scissors, so forcefully that it tears through the paper.

When the cartoon needs to be born, he reaches deep into his pocket where nothing was before and suddenly brandishes her two pink legs.

Is the mother of a cartoon always a cartoon, and is the world a cartoon lives in always a cartoon? Is her house a cartoon, and who put it here? She considers the round lake in her backyard, where the lure is a native species, and wonders who stocks it with white hands that reach up from beneath.

She is near the equator; it never freezes. And no more children will fall through the ice.

> She remembers how her heart hammered as she watched him. If the heart is a long hammering, then it stops when finally the picture will hang.

Say: the equator is a cartoon, the barest line of a person. It reaches into its coat and pulls out a round bomb, snowing white sparks at both poles.

The barest line is the enemy, the line cannot be killed, the line has who-knows-what up its sleeve. It says hit me as hard as you can, and watch the stars come out.

And she does, and they do, and under them, she dreams that the house will not let her build it. She dreams that she raises the frame and it falls. She raises the frame and it falls, and she raises the frame and it falls. So she dips a straight line in sugar and hangs it in the middle of the air, and the house grows in great crystals out of it, and stands.

And the line her enemy walks into the house, and closes the lines of the door behind him, and says put a hole through me.

My last coin, she sighs, and sends it through him.
And asks what does it buy?

And when he gives no answer, she takes him by the ankle, and holds him upside down and shakes him, and watches the following fall out:

GOOD CLIMBING TREES GROW US

And grow us up, deeper into the hand–
and the heart-shaped leaves. Here is how it happens:
       a baby is born either early or late in the fork
       of a mulberry tree, nudity sits on her skin
like a silkworm disease, longing for the world
leaps out of her silk glands, and attaches her
       to it; or a baby is born in the V of a tree
       and the light is a lapful of limes; or a baby
       is born where a live branch ends and as soon
       as she wonders what dangles her—as soon
as a stem extends upward—she grows peach skin
all over her body. Now ask how the babies learn:

literature opens among the leaves like so many
seed catalogues—it helps you decide what you
want, say the babies, and wait for what they want
       to come, mostly mango hairs and redfree,
or breadfruit for the religious, or cross between
       that and that, or the calm surface of a pond-
       apple, or a worm wearing glasses emerging
from them. When the leaves are the size of human

ears then the fruit is fully grown, and inside the house
       that owns the tree a human is spread on a chair,
the latest seed catalogue spread on her lap, her legs
like long yes columns, like long straight columns
of checks next to each kind of fruit in the world,
and she walks on them out to the tree and climbs
and grows shorter the higher she goes, and her checks
       and her yeses all drop off and hang heavy
       from the branches, and she climbs past the hand-
       and the heart-shaped, and she reaches the top
       with no other
       sweet left and says Goo in the loquat tree.

THE SALESMEN OPEN THEIR TRENCHCOATS, ALL
FILLED WITH POSSIBLE NAMES FOR THE WATCH

We wait in the house for just the word.
Dictionary salesmen line up outside the only door
in the world, and talk their way inside, and ask to see
the Mr., and ask to see the Mrs. "Not here," we say,
"never here." The salesmen tighten their trenchcoats.
Their stomachs, we hear, are eating themselves.
A suggestion of something floats through the air
and hooks in the salesmen's nostrils, and tugs them
toward the table, where empty birds are waiting.
The salesmen open their mouths. Their teeth are all
black gaps, they sink them into drumsticks. "Now
music," they command, and the piano becomes all
pressed-down spaces. Their briefcases are dictionaries.
The salesmen set them open, they gleam with rows
                              of what could own us,

          and what will it be the salesmen ask.
          We have not slept in weeks, waiting,
          and somewhere in our faces, pouches
          bulge with money to buy the eye, but
          we stare and cannot choose, and then

we cannot choose "stairs," disaster: they thaw
and run like rivers, and salesmen bend down
to drink the snowmelt, and feel something
                    rise or fall inside them;

          we cannot choose "mathematician,"
          and he climbs in the bath and cries
          when displacement of water is less
          than himself; and we cannot choose

          "leopard," disaster: an approximate cat
          appears in our midst and gallops audibly
          toward us, patterned all over with leper
                    bells, crying, "Get close to me,"

and the wind of his country is at his back,
but we cannot choose "whoosh," disaster:
and wind goes with a final gust,
           rush of a thousand doors swung-to,

and the dictionary salesmen slam themselves
shut but lacking our "click" they cannot latch,
and their brass combinations swing free
           as they march away from us, and then

they are gone and we are glad. We lay ourselves
out in state and wait for them to come again: an hour
straight here and a solid month there lay bricks against
the bricks. Next year we will be ready. Next year we will
spend the money—if their green is the same as our green.
The oldest boy was next in line, but now at night our mother
opens her only book, trails a finger down the list of begats,
thinks how a small name continued, from head to hip
to toe, its babylineal descent, till finally it dropped
out of him. And his grass became our green. And now
at night we sleep on piles
                      of endless independent means.

THE CONSTRUCTION OF A FOREST FOR THE STAGE

Last week we built the inside of a mountain
for the stage, next week we will build the inside
of a wolf, but now we must go walking in the wood
and find the tallest veneer tree, and fell it, and ride it
downstream and straight through red curtains,
and saw it thinner than paper, and stand the look
of a forest up. If a woman lives in the forest, we build
her a half-log cabin out of only the visible sides
of trees. She is self-sufficient; in her hand, the play
opens out like a hundred-blade jackknife, and
she cuts her name, and then all of us are watching:

a fossil wind stands stone around everything,
filled with feather and fern imprints. The forest
        is in a foreign country, all animals are possible
        here, and all possible animals begin to appear.
The stage directions say: "The 'forest' is full of eyes,"
and the stage directions say: "The 'forest' is full of all
fours." They say, "Black and white masks float back
and forth," and they say, "All moths fly in pairs around
here; the display of one moth requires two moths."
They say, "You see bright beetles," and the people
are forced to picture them: they break out into life
like beads on their upper lips, or gather themselves
like blood along a cut, or button themselves into the world
        and then, in order to die, pop violently off the belly
        of a third-row man in a black tuxedo.
        They say, "Sit up in your chairs,

your uprightness is a specimen pin." Uprightness
climbs the trees like vines. They say, "The woman
appears, the woman is wearing a little green shimmer,
like where a gorilla has crashed through the leaves."
The directions say it is set in the place "where parallelism
grows, where straight trees grow up on the straight-
        down rain." It is winter, and even the animals
        are lean as arrow meat; up, there are no stars,

but radiant staples flash in the script, and the folded
paper problem reaches to the moon, and the play closes
like a hundred-blade jackknife, and she dies. And who
          could say what happened. The audience files out
one by one, they are red-eyed, they are ragged where
their tickets were torn off, and as soon as they are gone,
we are flattening the set and we are stacking it and we

          are building the inside of a skull for the stage—
                    and outside, according to the law of skulls,
                              a face is light enough to read print by.

THE FRONT HALF AND THE BACK HALF OF
A HORSE IN CONVERSATION

"We both read for the part, and both of us were chosen,
    and we were buttoned into the horse together,
    baggy in the middle and as plodding as a novel.
    Our stage mother sewed the suit, she made it red
with white ankles, to give the impression of a solid horse."
The director is a famous eccentric with his name on the back
of his chair; he speaks to the horse through a silver cone,
says More or Less or Louder, more froth on the flanks
or more rolling eyes. Tonight is dress rehearsal;
the horse shakes a hand heartily inside itself
and wishes itself good luck. "Are you galloping
hard in all your parts?" the front half asks the back,
and they take their first step forward, powered
                            with plunging stomachs.
Silence. "Who will make our Clop-Clop noise?"
the back half asks the front, who opens either hand
to show a horseshoe and a cobblestone, the cobblestone
warm and almost throbbing, desiring to rise in the center
of a puddle and have a hoof set squarely on it. The horse
makes a single entrance, and a ripple of delight goes over
the crowd. "Get closer to me," the front half hisses, "our spine
is broken again." They wrap their arms around each other.
"Will you feed me my lines if I forget?" the back half asks
the front, then remembers they have no lines at all.
"Of course I will," the front half says, "I'll fork lines
over you like hay." They pretend to sleep in a corner,
with a lasso looped around their neck. Then the lasso
starts to tighten, and old scenery tiptoes off, and a spotlight
                            shines a silver lake on the horse

continuum. That's the cue for them to wade, and three sheer
lengths of silk begin to billow across the stage, green,
blue, and lavender, with water-striders dragging
snags behind them. The line of the lasso goes taut,
and both halves of the horse splash forward,
and the front plunges all its hooves, and the back
plunges all its hooves. Horse-eyes roll in their horse-

holes. The director's mouth makes a perfect O
inside the silver cone. The front half can read lips, and nods.
He needs to tell the back half, but he can't remember his lines—
"eccentric..." "eccentric dot dot dot..."

All water in the world is silk
now, and the world is the same in every way except two words
are switched: concentric for eccentric, and nothing else
is different:

"What a concentric man we say, and his outlines
all surround each other as if he'd been hit
with a hammer, or what a concentric hat we say,
and it's easy to see how a skipping stone
made it, and that she is underwater, and rich people
are concentric, we say, and pour smaller
and smaller circles through fingers all the while
laughing out loud,

or dog owners are concentric we say,
and we see them walking empty collars all over
the streets of the town, and stopping to let them
sniff circles around stumps of sawn-down trees,
or cat owners are concentric, and we see them on all
fours, lapping milk out of little saucers, and I'm a bit
of a concentric myself we say and lift a widening
monocle to one of our eyes;"

And the line floods back to the front half, it is:
The famous concentric is shouting Big Splash!
And the line washes over the back half, who takes
a breath and holds it, who closes his eyes and sees
the page and reads what it tells him to do, {HORSE
STOOMP HIS SILVER HOOF}, all concentricities of the text
preserved, and he acts it to the letter, and he acts the extra
O, and he lifts his hoof and sets it down and nails it
to a ringing shoe.

THE QU

KENING

THE QUICKENING

The boy takes a day at the beach. He walks to the end of the pier and drops his line in the water. Just the flash on a hook, no worm, and he waits.

The boy does not fish for fish, but fishes for the moment when the line goes live, and fishes for the Nibble. He hauls the nibble in and lets it gasp in the middle of the air, and then drops it down his throat and swallows it raw.

The nibble slides visibly down the throat of the boy—visibly because a whale is watching. "Delicious," says the boy, and "Delicious!" cries the whale. She leaps out of the water and swallows him whole, the moment when the line goes live still swimming toward his stomach, and down they go together into the deep.

And the bottom of the sea is so far away, it eats most of a day to swim there.

Meanwhile the boy swims down the endless throat of the whale, and just when the whale arrives at the bottom of the sea, the boy is spilled out into the belly of the whale.

At the same moment, feels a silver splash in his own stomach.

And wonders what the nibble has inside it—the twitch of a fly, perhaps.

He is still alive; he has not passed into history. It could have been worse, he thinks. I could have been swallowed by the written whale, the Orca.

The boy treads water and looks around him. Great dunes of flesh slope down the whale's insides to meet the sea, and hundreds of red jellyfish are washed up on them. There are tidepools where the dunes turn rocky; they are full of purple urchins, and anemones open and close there.

The horizon is streaked with cirrus fat and sunset colors. Above, night is falling, and hundreds of harpoons went home in her. The points leap out of her dome, and hang stars of perfect sharpness all over the firmament of the whale.

There are enough of them to see by, and they shine light on a shipwreck in the middle of the ocean. A houseboat went to sea while a storm was blowing—it always hated to be indoors—and now it resembles nothing so much as a sea of rooftops seen from above. The boy swims out toward it, and finds flints and steel, and coils of rope, and boxes of candles, and a tin of sardines. A potbelly stove gleams in the darkness, with a falling-down shack of firewood inside. A birdcage dangles from the ceiling, but there is no bird, only yellow sections of Daily Bugle.

There is a writing desk in one corner, with the inkwell still full, and a hammock hanging in the other.

A smaller slap of waves seems to follow him through the cabin; the boy looks high and low and discovers a half-empty canteen. He slings it over his shoulder and listens to it slosh.

Thinks, "I can live here—many people live on the backs of sleeping whales, and are only plunged under when they try to light a fire." And lights a fire.

He peers over the side of the shipwreck, and sees that the tumble down the whale broke his nose. It goes crooked now down the middle of his face, like a diverted stream.

"Or a man looks down one morning and sees his bed sitting on top of a waterspout. How is this any different?"

The boy climbs into the hammock and lets the shipwreck rock him to sleep. The hammock needs mending; he bursts out of it like 153 fish, like the catch called up to prove a point.

His body is all belly when he wakes. The sardines are arranged in rows of seven. He lifts a Monday by the tail and swallows it, and washes it down with a long pull from his canteen. Looks toward the empty birdcage. "Daily Bugle, are you thirsty?" And pours a little water on the news, to keep it living.

He didn't mean to ask out loud—oh God, did the whale hear? The boy holds his breath for a long minute, and then shouts, "I was meant to speak; the human body is a podium, a pitcher of water, and a drinking glass." And rests his hand on his canteen.

The whale keeps her hearing in her jaw, and her whole mouth fills up with the boy's speech, and the whole ton of her thrums with gladness. She chews and swallows a huge HELLO, and it comes flying down inside her and splashes in the water.

"Are you all there?" asks the whale. "Are you still him, are you still a He?"

The boy opens his lips and no sound comes out. Every line on his face adds a year to his life.

The whale spreads her flippers wide. "Please don't be afraid. Think of me simply as a Great Fish, as a catch-all term made flesh."

The boy hides under the writing desk and does not answer. The whale lurches forward and sends him skidding out into the open.

"Will you talk to me?" she pleads. "I can pay you."

"How do you pay, in cowries?"

"I can pay you in cowries," says the whale, "or I can pay you in small Notes."

And the whale begins to count them out; as long as you are reading this counts them out.

This whale is an intellectual, she has designed a book that even whales can read; a book that surrounds them.

"Look! And me a licked thumb between the pages."

"What writes it?" he asks, and already knows the answer: whitemargins and dottybacks, as far as the eye can see.

"Let me be school for you," begs the whale. "Let me be a one-room schoolhouse, and teach all of your ages at once."

She opens the book and reads, "I caught an enormous fish," and savors the words in her mouth, and her cheek grows around a sudden hook, and trails line from it.

"More," says the boy, and the whale swims to the spitting surface and reads ᷉᷉᷉᷉᷉᷉ . The boy bursts into applause; he bends down and slaps the water with his hands.

"In school—in my school," he suggests, "we do Addition and Subtraction after Reading." The whale feels a sudden deep pity for him, and tells him to dive into the water. The boy dives into his reflection and then surfaces, and sees the water filled with ripples, with approximately equal signs.

"A book was once written about me," the whale says shyly; "it was very famous, they titled it *Fat Blue Volume*. If I was a blue whale before, I am a black-and-white whale now."

> This gives the boy a moment of hope. "Will there be a second edition?" he asks himself. "If it includes an exploding diagram, then I can be outside the whale again."

"The book says," the whale bursts out, "that I am the heaviest organ in the world's body: not the heart, not the brain, but the skin of it." The boy shudders violently at the thought, and the shudder runs under the skin of the whale.

They swim always in a cold current; seawater strokes over them. "Are we going faster?" the boy asks, and she says, "Before you came, I swam at a speed of one knot per hour. Now that you're here, I can go two knots at last."

When the boy puts out his fire at bedtime, a whale of darkness fills the whale, and all night long, it eats the worms that eat shade plants.

> During the day, the whale of darkness lives outside the whale, the shape of it small on the ocean floor.*

> > *Not like the shadow of a boy on earth, which is blood pouring out of a pant leg.

The boy gazes up through the roof of the houseboat, and looks for constellations among the stars of perfect sharpness. Stares up through empty space and breathes and sees only the Air Pump and the Sea Monster.

Next morning he swallows a Tuesday and a Wednesday, and then a whole week of sardines, and starts to worry. Ties a Sunday to a line and drops it in the water, but it drifts and stays slack. If worse comes to worst, he figures, he can always gather mussels in the tidepools of the whale.

> And as long as a freshwater lake is inside him, the nibble is still alive—it has not turned into a Death Throe yet.

His own body is still intact so far. Is all of me digestible? he wonders, and pictures the whale coughing up a tidy packet of what is not—molars and ulnas, his broken nose-bone, a pocket containing one fish skeleton in sandstone, two hooks, a length of line, and an anchor button waiting to be sewed back on.*

*The boy reaches into his pocket to jangle these odds and ends, and finds a pair of magnets also. He takes the magnets out and lets them repel each other, he feels force firm as a grape between them, and pops it into his mouth.

A seagull is trapped inside with him. It wheels among the stars of perfect sharpness, and pecks from time to time at the sunset of the whale. The boy understands—he remembers how the last pink slither of the sun used to wiggle along the horizon, and then something leaped out of him to swallow it, and it was gone.

But how did the gull get here? "I landed on the back of the whale, and took one beakful and then another, and somehow couldn't stop, and ate the whale inside out."

A bird that flew into his classroom one day during Silent Reading is trapped here too. It flies only in his field of vision, and nests in the hair that falls over his eyes, and seems to grow bigger and bigger.

And finally the boy bends his head, and it dives for his last sardine.

A field trip to the seashore is in here, and the week of anticipation is in here, and the boy who got lost there is in here too. An early obsession with Lake Michigan is in here, and its shores of polished Petoskey stones. His newspaper kite is in here, and his struggle with the kite string. His spiral Vocabulary notebook is in here, and trouble telling the difference between the Atlantic and the Pacific, and a spanking that he got for eating mercury, and a collection of 100 dimes all stamped the year he was born. The Presidency of the Fossil Hunter's Club is in here, and how he longed to find a femur of anything. A chapter of *News of the World* is in here: "America Swallows the Mermaid Hoax!" A shoebox diorama of the Chugwater Formation is in here, with flecks of mica and flakes of quartz shining between the layers, and its lack of a skeleton still in mid-swim is gleaming in here too.

His year in the school orchestra is in here, when it was his job to raise a hand high and bring it down boom on a drum, and make the sound a cartoon makes when it gulps down something good.

His jump-rope record of 24 continuous jumps is in here too, like 24 ribs of the whale.

The whale asks, "Aren't you happy at all? Think of the cramped handwriting you left behind, how it lives in a boardinghouse with low stained ceilings, how a train goes by day and night, how the walls are thin as you-know-what."

"How do you know my handwriting?" The boy closes his eyes and tries to remember it; he looks out at the waves and sees it slanting to the right. "You used to chew scraps of your notes," the whale says tenderly. "Your small gray spitballs fly through my blowhole all day and all night long."

And the boy feels a sudden substance in his mouth, and the stub of a pencil behind one ear.

What does a whale see, and how does she see it? Picture this: her eyes are holes on either side of her head. Long yellow pencils are sharpened into them, and the shavings fall down inside her and settle on the roof of the houseboat and the surface of the water.

"Your sight is nothing like that," says his own inhabitant. "It leaps into you in arcs, like sudden leaks sprung in the body of a boat." "Hush," the boy tells him, and gathers up the shavings, and burns them in the belly of the stove and sees by them.

He lost his clothes on the way down, and shivers in front of the fire. He imagines himself in a sailor shirt, with a clean white page down the back, and imagines himself in a fisherman's sweater with coarse round holes all over it, so that his skin shines through in a Rare Coin Display.

"How are you feeling?" wonders the whale. "Stand straight as spume and let me look at you." The boy stands straight for a wavering second, then falls down in dollar-sized droplets. The whale shakes her head, and pays out another note like a length of line:

> The boy licks away a tear. "Is Digestion beginning, now, tonight? Is your empty belly breaking me down?" She says, "I'm not empty at all, tonight;"

> and ends on a semicolon, and a gibbous pause rises into the sky and hangs there instead of a moon.

The sunset colors glow hotter, and the days blur into each other, and his appearance begins to bead on him like sweat, and his appearance begins to peel off in long sheets and strips. His sleep becomes feverish—he dreams he is curled up on the whale's tongue, inside a great rough rose of a tastebud.

As dry as his own mouth is, he spits on all the brightwork of his shipwreck every morning, and polishes until he can see his face.

In another dream, the whale is an impossible bottle, and the boy is lying flat on his back inside, with a long string tied to his toe. He feels a tug on the string, and his body begins to unfold into masts and rigging and bellying sails.

All the nails of his houseboat are working their way out and falling tap-tap into the water. The boy wishes for a hammer—any hammer, a reflex hammer—to pound them in again.

His first visit to the doctor is in here: hundredth percentile in weight, hundredth percentile in height, and lit up with vital signs. "He'll grow into that massive head," laughs the doctor, and that is in here too.

There is less and less fresh water. The boy and the whale grow quiet, and make confessions to each other. "I have never seen myself," the whale says. "What do I look like?" It has been so long since the boy has seen anything. He looks around at his shipwreck. "Like a sea of rooftops seen from above."

"I felt full of angles once, all blue facets and faces, before the water wore me smooth," and she smiles a curving smile.

The boy nods. "The first night I spent at the seashore, I never fell asleep—I thought there was a huge rock tumbler outside my window; that it roared at me all night long; that it turned over and over around a rough chunk of turquoise."

They play games to pass the time. When the whale leaps out of the water with the boy in her belly, she leaps in two parts, like a game of checkers.

> When checkers are green and blue instead of red and black, they are a game about the ocean and not a game about the war.

"Am I your first animal?" asks the whale. The boy answers, "I had a horse but I never rode him—I rode the moment when the horsefly landed, and rode the little ripple that ran under the horse's skin."

"I try to keep pets, but they never last," says the whale. "When I was small, I brought home a blue eye that swam in a fishbowl, and fed it every day. Then I brought home another, and they ate each other."

Drops of the boy's appearance fall splashing onto the floor. "Can you try to understand me?" pleads the whale. "If you were a saltwater tank, you would want a little shipwreck, a deep-sea diver, and a gold-spilling chest to display in you too."

"Display to who?" asks the boy. The whale dips into the book that surrounds them, and turns to *Six Characters in Search of an Author*. "Listen to this," she begins, and the boy notices, for the first time, a chalk x on the stage of the shipwreck.

While she reads, the boy steps onto his mark and stands there, and swallows the last of his water. "Is that a true story?" he asks, and she nods. "I know this for a fact: somewhere out there is a room full of women who do nothing but draw bubbles for this ocean."

"I toured the Aquarium once," says the boy. "The fish there never eat, only open their mouths against the inside of the glass."

"What else?" the whale asks, suddenly hungry.

"The oldest guide never goes home. He sleeps among the tanks, he draws the shadow of a ray up to his chin, he burbles a word from time to time. He has internalized three speeches, from outside in: Boat Scars, Whales, Boys."

The belly heaves a sigh. "Why would you want to stay up there? Live long, get sick, take cobalt."

The next morning, out of nowhere, the gull swoops down and pecks out his eyes, and replaces them with his first sight of the sea.

And that night, when the stars of perfect sharpness are all out and shining, the whale is unusually quiet. "What are you reading?" the boy asks, and the whale looks in at him, and laments her lack of tear glands, and turns her eyes out and reads:

I.

He grows ears, eyes, and arms in the belly of the whale;
he grows a way to be looked at; grows a broken nose
at the age of nine; grows an empty stomach, grows pieces
of pepper between the teeth; grows a third-grade education;
grows The Gettysburg Address; grows first the bones
of the hand, then grows recitation of the bones of the hand;
grows a pregnant teacher; grows the openness of jaws
at the local museum; grows his favorite text: "Am I a sea,
or a whale, that thou settest a watch over me?" Grows
h-e-i-g-h-t-h in his spelling bee;

> then grows his grown up,
> his gone to sea and grows
> his own Gone Missing;

II.

He washes the mouth of the whale; he swims toward
one unit of candlelight; he sleeps on a shipwreck inside
the whale and sends his smoke to the breathing roof;
he eats year-old bread in the belly of the whale
and the whale's hunger does not diminish, how?
he eats fat rudderfish in the belly of the whale and
the whale's hunger goes nowhere, how and how?
and slowly, he loses his way to be looked at; he grows
a way to be read at breakfast; he grows a Y and a fine
white spray;

> he grows his final words, "Watch, the eye
> of the whale will swallow you also."

The whale closes the book, and the boy closes his first sight of the sea. He lifts up his canteen and drinks the last of the empty out of it, and stares sadly at Daily Bugle. "The paper isn't delivered here," he says. "If I had died, we wouldn't know it." And then zzzzzz, he falls asleep. A fly rises out of the inkwell and lands at the corner of his mouth.

> He dreams that he and the whale surface together. A fly buzzes and lands on the whale, and the boy rides the little shudder that runs under her skin. And digs his heels into it, faster, faster, and makes it leap.

And the heart of the boy stops inside the whale, and a visible swallow goes down the throat of the world.

CHILDREN WITH LAMPS POURING OUT OF THEIR FOREHEADS

Descend into the fact mine. We are here because
we failed fifth grade, we could not pass the bone unit,
we tried to pry up "greenstick fracture" and pried
"greenhouse fracture" up instead, it seemed logical
at the time, we saw panes of glass bursting out
of their frames because someone threw a stone,
        and after class we told the teacher, "Children
        were being children, and one of them threw
a stone," and our arms hung strangely in our sleeves,
and she said, "Line up at the door, and lob yourselves
into the earth, and find what kind of stone it was,"

                and now we are sentenced to mine—
not the stones themselves, but the color of their streaks,
what scratches them and what they scratch, industrial uses,
drillbit uses, music-extracting uses. We are mining where
                they are typically found.

        There is a gleam on each of them, like the small
        yellow bird on the clean of a hippo tooth. As for us
        we have no canaries, but a superscript hovers near
        each head, th or nd or nth or st, they make our mere
        numbers into Birthdates, our birthdates dart down
        ahead of us and test whether we can live there,

        and of course we can, and we make our way, bent
almost in half by huge ceiling crystals of what stunts human
growth. We practice room and pillar mining; we cut palaces
out exactly, each room we cut out is a study and the kinds
        of columns hold them up, and the kinds of marble
        make the columns, and the methods of polishing
make them shine. Then we move into the ore rooms,
one painted scratchoff silver with immutable numbers
underneath, one wavy with banded iron, like a spelling
workbook dropped in the bath; then into the rubify
room, where it means "make ruby red," but a dash

is missing somewhere; then into the brilliant
cut room, where Fancy Deep Grayish Blue Facts are held out,
                    surrounded by glinting quote marks,

        and the deeper we go the more we are the diamonds,
surrounded by sharp intakes of breath. Long years of breathing
the air down here have given us lung complaints: if sea stars are
all lung and tarantulas have four lungs, how can two be enough
for a Walking-Talking? Yet two is enough and two is a fact;
we cough and feel stabbing pains, we feel our own pickaxes
        strike down inside us and pry up our chunks of pink
        quartz, and we spit. We cannot be absent for the test—
the test is today, and the test is tomorrow. Flashcards

            show all of their sides at once. Now when
a fracture jumps out of our frame, we know the right
word for it—a note is wrapped around the stone,
it says you belong to me now, it says stay where
        you are, stay deep in the possessive pronoun.
It says I watch through your window, morning to noon
to night. The fact of our eyes is surrounded with squint,
we read the note over and over. The bone that we break
is the Radius, and points. And around it, arrayed in shine lines,
                    all the minutes of the day.

THE CHURCH OF THE OPEN CRAYON BOX

Must be entered through the sharpener every Sunday,
else your name will be lovingly written in the Book
of the Down Arrow. The One Steeple to Every Church
                    rule breaks in half
in the Church of the Open Crayon Box; the One Bell
to Every Steeple rule breaks off its tip. "Climb stairs
to the steeples," the preacher commands, "and let
every belltone ring out!" You can see the whole town
            from the steeple, and you exit the church through
            the view, and you walk through what calls itself

                    Flagpole—the town is a blot
                    on the town, but the railroad
is coming out this way and we must give them a smear
to see through the windows: now you pass the General Store,
that even your vaguest stick figure can enter, now you pass
a vacant lot: the post office isn't here yet, is only a set-aside space
in the center of the country's envelope; now you pass the voting-
place, where we stuff our handwriting through a slit. Tall trees
fall in the pinewoods, tall telegraph poles are raised, and words
inch along our wires: text text text stop, text text text stop.

And now you pass the Feed Store, which sells carrot and turnip
and sugar-beet tops—only the visible parts—and now Whitey
BaLavender's Hardware, where everything hangs off the hook
of its color, or color hangs off the hook of its all, where you work
your hands into cool washers, and work hands into nailheads
of the color blue, and watch Whitey BaLavender busy himself
            pouring crayons into bullet molds. You show him a list
            that says "ax," and he sells you a red line through it.
                    All up and down Main Street ponies are covered
                    with strokes as coarse as horse blankets. And once
            you have drawn the ponies you begin to draw the saddle
shop, you grip the right color like a saddle horn and somehow
keep from falling off, and you ride to the edge of town,

where you draw the fur trading post, where they sell tails
of any shy animal, the rest of the animal gone down a hole,
where you trade in your skin for a possibles bag and wear
possibles bag where your skin was. Fat geese fly in any letter
you like but you need red meat for once, and write a splayed-
hide word like "Deerslayer," and take hold of the ending
                              and drag it home,

and now you are almost there, now you are building the home
with hand-drawn Log Cabin Font, you are building it log
by log of course and smoothing the logs with a color called
Adze, you are biting the crayon to notch the logs and driving
in dots of nailheads. Stumps of umber surround you, and the sky
is beginning to look like sky. You are hoping a man can be really
          alone here;
                    you are hoping your father can tell what it is;
and now only the doorknob is left to draw and in your enthusiasm
you shout at the paper, and the weather
                    changes just in time, not raining, beginning to spit.

THE FATHER OF THE FICTIONAL ALPHABET

Hovers over his invention, all spirals and lightbulbs and
whistles and bells, all knobs and dials and black balloons,
blinking panels and pinwheels, whirs and beeps and flying
signals, doors with smaller doors behind them, cuckoos
        on juicy steel springs, mechanical catfish whiskers
trembling in currents of air, machine-made exhalations,
        tuba polish for booming parts and trombone polish
for pumping parts. Mirror polish for mirror letters and
sunken brass for silent ones
                and readout pours from every single slot.

The letters must be forged—the father of the fictional alphabet
wears protective glasses, and holds flat and round sounds
in the roaring fire and uses a seashell for flux, and then drops
each letter in a bowl of cool water, and they steam in the shape
        of themselves, and the father of the fictional alphabet
rivets them to the machine: on all sides, in brass letters, it says;

                and it belches black smoke and itself,
and white mice run in wheels inside it, a clearie marble
rolls down a track, and here is a slot for quarters where
you buy a *chgnk chgnk* sound. The letters have whirligigs
in them, the letters release hundreds of helicopters, the letters
have snakes that slip between stones, the letters grow parrot-
head flowers, and the letters are bodies settled with blackflies.
                        Why all the
nature metaphors—the needles here are slammed to green
as if the machine is a habitat, and the needles here are slammed
to red as if the machine is tooth and claw.
                        He had an assistant, a finger
quoter, who saw her best fingers fly off. It must be said she cried;
all her letters grew bulges at every end and these were called
their Teardrop Terminals. Her quotes turned black and came to life
and tiptoed through the works, flipped first/last letters everywhere
                        and not a single on/off

switch. The father misses her. The father is running on steam.
He takes off his glasses and breathes in the lenses and returns
the stems to his face. The machine breaks down and he gets it
humming. He is nearly a letter himself now, he hangs
            a Teardrop Terminal off the sad end of his nose.
                              Ribbons of paper pour out and out,
covered with endless addition. The World Exposition
is tomorrow, and the father of the fictional alphabet
is ready to raise the curtain;
                              he lifts the last letter and locks it in place
                    with the last Universal Head Rivet, now look.

They are indigenous in me, says Old green America.
The law says go west, and pick a plot of land, and build
an 8x10 house under shade of my law, and live there,
       and the title of the land will stream into your fingers.
The country is still so new, the states must draw themselves
every morning, all real and future and possible states
draw themselves over the land. "This country is infested
with states," say the settlers, "they crawl on their bellies
through the mud, have learned to look like their surroundings,
eat other states and their own young. They suffer like spiders
from ingrown silk; their backs are marked with one white star."

      We were counterfeiters before and have paper left over,
      so we turn all our eyes to the west. The law never grew
      a dimension mark and Old green America never said "feet,"
      so we draw plans for 8x10 inch houses. We'll paint them
      miniature white, and pose with one boot on the roof,
            and wait for our land to come rolling in;

yet somehow our plans are never finished, a new west wall
always wants to be added, each window wants a confetti bush.
We draw deeper and deeper into the house, the house grows
over with flourishes. Before too long we add people: inside
the people drink miniature water while miniature sunshine
      pours through the glass and fractions of seconds tick by.
Inside the people are dots, they eat fictional inches added
to fish, they stumble outside every morning and haul small
reflections up from their wells. All pigs there are in-pig
which is to say pregnant, and their trapdoor spiders fall
through themselves. The wife soothes the cow as it makes
a copy, and skims cream-colored stationery off her milk.
When she wants a flock of chickens, her children all outline
their hands, and a flock of chickens appears. When she wants
      to kill one, she sets it loose

and it runs itself to death
on the family piano: it plays high to low and low to high
and then races up and past the keyboard and keeps
playing for a moment in the air—even shapes
· of chickens don't know when they're dead.

It's the year of smallest statehood, the people lie down
on the floor to sleep, the states sneak in through any crack
and draw faithfully around them while they dream, draw
North on one and South on the other, and then the states
crawl into their mouths and draw where they will wake up
tomorrow, and stand with one state
in each foot of you,
laughing, and North wakes and sees that South has been bitten,
and she bends down and sucks the green boundary out.

FIG. 1

Here is a picture of the author, here is the mother
of her mother, here is a picture of the family forehead,
which wrinkled and creased like the forehead of Literature,
here is the author trapped in a classroom, with her grammar
open in front of her face. Here is the author's pet wasp,

who had a straight line for a stinger, who perched on her finger
as she wrote; here is a picture of her bedroom wall, where she made
a slash mark every day, and because she was religious, a diagonal
slash on Sundays. Here is the author in her kitchen, grinding
whole punctuation into little pepper. Here is the author

in her garden, laying fat fig.s out to dry, and here is the author's
backyard, where the alphabet grew straight up until an animal
came along, and she learned to read the bent-down grass; here
is a picture of her favorite tree, full of a single black-and-white fruit,
and here is a picture of black-and-white juice smeared on her smiling
                          chin. Lightning flashed and the favorite tree

fell open to the death scene, and she took an ax and hacked
until she had a sticky door, and she hung it by two hinges
and it yielded every year. Here is a picture of her writing desk,
which had an elbow for her elbow, and here is a picture
of her pencil cup, that she sometimes tried to drink from—
believing herself to be lost in the desert—and here is a page
of notes that reads:

FIG. I

        Is a picture of the author in profile, writing a desert
through her window. She stares at the sand and prays
        for no rain, since too much rain makes the fig.
            split. Lines ray away from the author, they
are labeled A B C. Now she walks into her garden and bends
down the grass, now she lets the grass trail off and she lets
the sand begin, now she steps and leaves fresh tracks,
in the hope that a following animal
                believes fresh tracks

to be fig.s, in the hope that a following animal will eat
and excrete them somewhere else. She begins to suffer
from exposure. What will I drink? she wonders, and a cactus
stands up against the sky, and what will I eat, she wonders,

        and the fruit of a succulent is straight lines,
        and her pet wasp lands on her longest finger
            and sees the end coming and stings her with it.

ACKNOWLEDGMENTS

I would like to thank the editors of the following magazines, in which versions of these poems originally appeared: *AGNI, Everyday Genius, Hayden's Ferry Review, MAKE, New Orleans Review, PANK, Poetry, Poetry Northwest, Rattle, Seattle Review* and *West Wind Review.*